RANCH PICKERS YARD SALE

4735 S. ENGLEHART AVE. REEDLEY 93654

**NOVEMBER 17TH, 18TH, & 19TH
THURSDAY, FRIDAY, & SATURDAY
6:AM to 2:PM
EARLY BIRDS WELCOME**

We are excited about our fall yard sale, and can't wait to see you all again! NEW STUFF DAILY. COME EARLY & BRING A TRUCK. We have large & small furniture, up-cycle materials, tools, rusty stuff & JUNK. hand painted signs, crafty stuff, kitchen & home decor, doors, windows, antiques, vintage, SEASONAL STUFF, FREE COFFEE. It's always a surprise. See you in NOVEMBER!

PLEASE: NO PETS. and bring someone to help you load if possible. PREVIEW on INSTAGRAM the night before on wahtokecreek.

https://www.facebook.com/mywahtokecreek/

PosterMyWall.com

Welcome

The Ranch Pickers Yard Sale began two years ago. I had collected so many things in lots from auctions and needed an outlet for it. As I looked at the side yard I knew I needed to have a yard sale but didn't want to do it alone. I told my husband that it would be much more fun to invite our friends to participate. I had no idea how true that would be at the time. The first sale was so good we all decided to keep it going. Now, three times a year, we hold a sale to mark each season. During the months of April, August, and November, we pack the driveway and old garden area with treasures for someone else to find. It takes us all two days or more to get it set up. No one ever really knows what they'll find when they come out here. We tell everyone to come early and bring a truck. Each sale brings new surprises. Every morning we bring out new items to sell. We do this so the sale stays fresh for people that haven't been here before or for our returning shoppers from the previous day.

As our readers walk through these pictures we hope it sparks their unlimited imagination, creativity, and their curiosity as to what treasures the next sale may hold for them.

Stay tuned for the next Ranch Pickers Yard Sale in April of 2017. And thank you in advance for coming out. We know it's going to be another amazing sale.

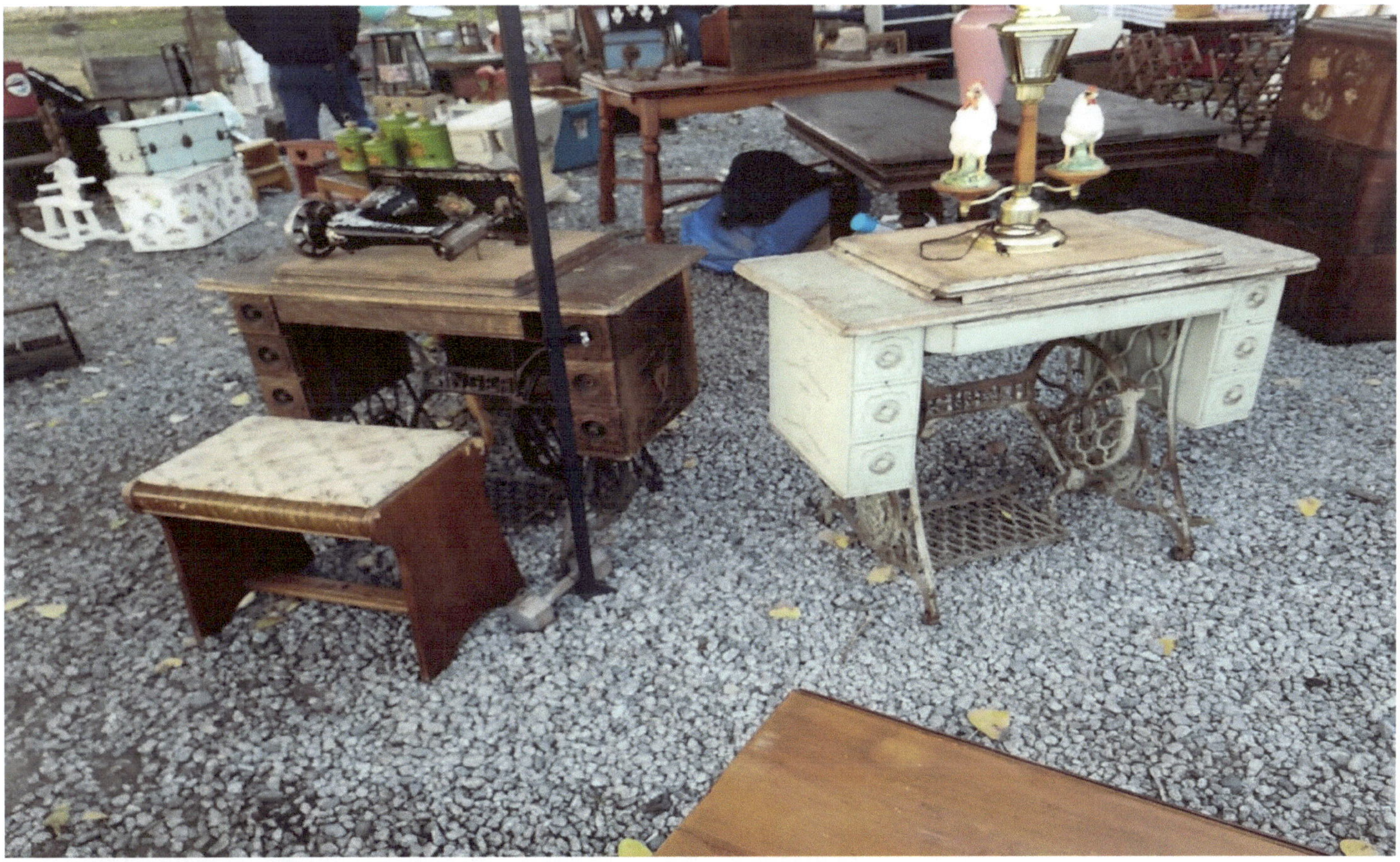

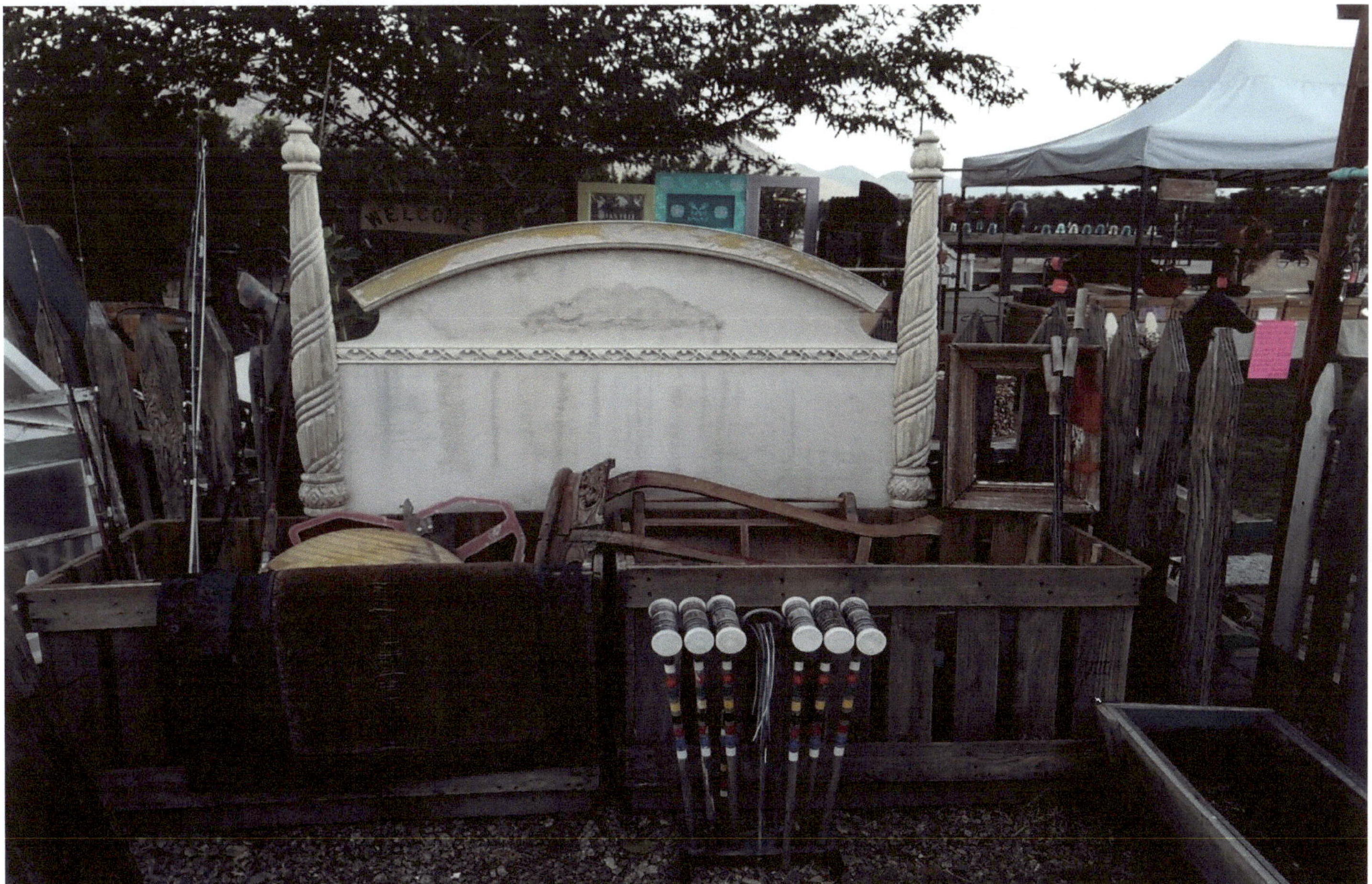

So many things to see

It's not just about the fun of the yard sale hunt. It's about sustainability. Just because something is old doesn't mean its worth becomes less. We live in a time where people want it "now." But, we must remember that the things we throw out for the new can still be used in some way. To sustain ourselves, our lifestyles, we need to take a second look at what we have around us. Think twice about what gets thrown out. Where is out? Does it really go away? Everything must go somewhere.

Re-Purpose ~ Re-Use

~ Red~

Is the color used for every season.

We use it in our fall arrangements, Christmas décor, and for color in our spring and summer flower gardens. Red is a warm, bright festive color that can bring cheer to a room or patio.

~ Red is a Statement ~

Antique Childs fainting couch, needs to be reupholstered, all 4 casters present, all woodwork in good shape...asking $100.00
Visit Ranch Pickers Yard Sale on Facebook

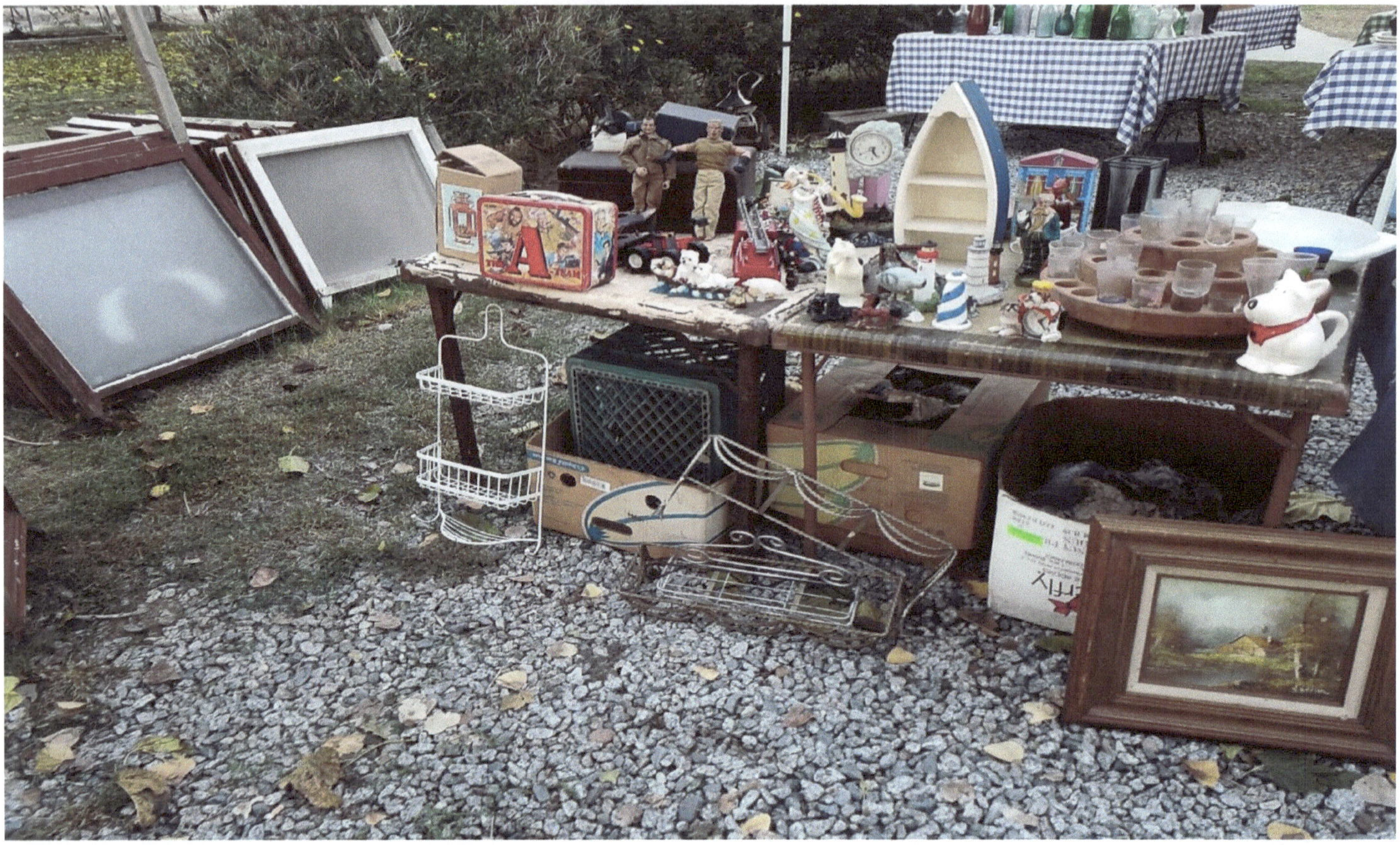

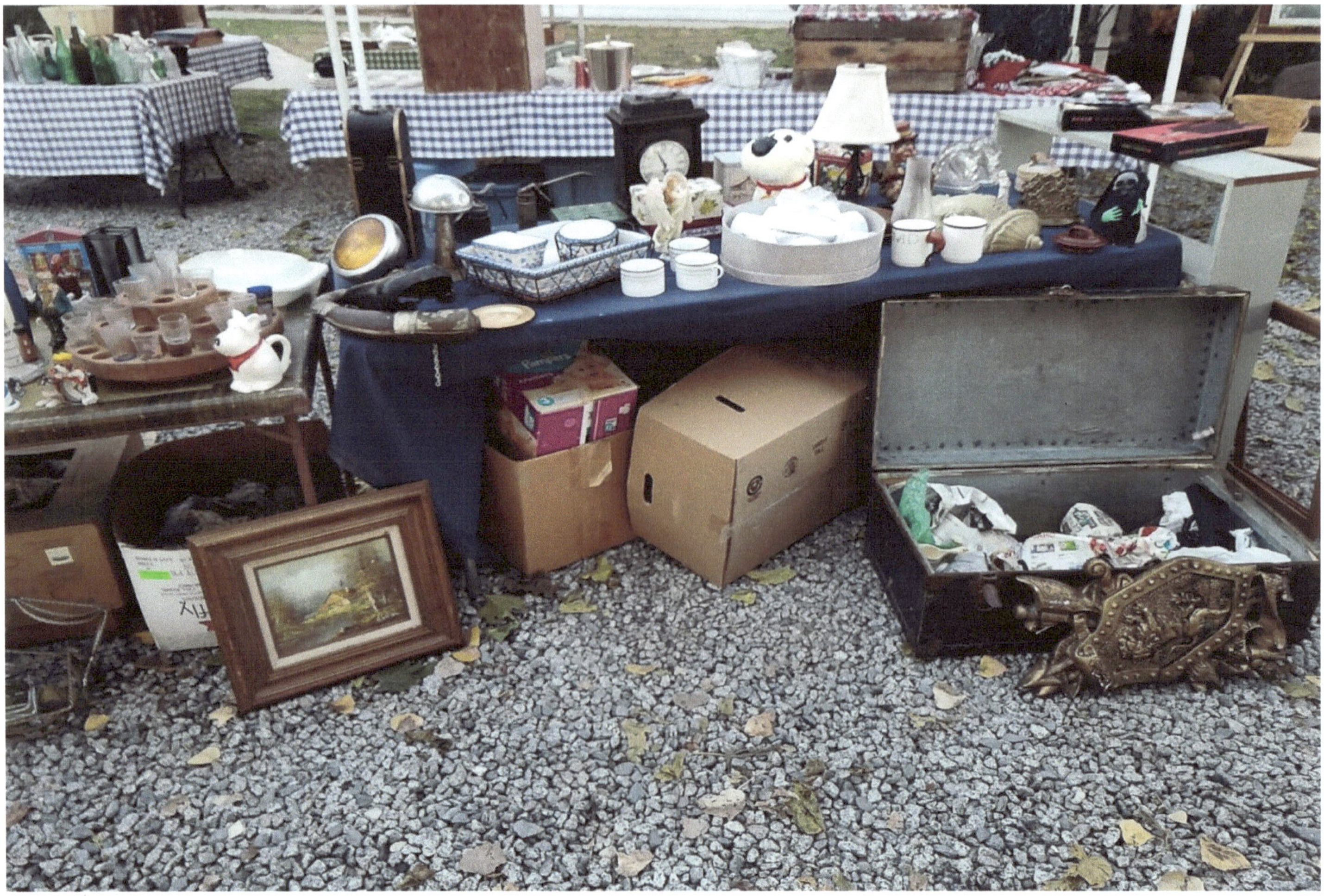

Thank You for visiting and shopping our Ranch Pickers Yard Sale

Stay tuned for information on the Spring 2017 Ranch Pickers Yard Sale

Our Ranch Pickers Yard Sale always has free coffee in the mornings, and sometimes one of us picks up the donuts. We look forward to all the early birds no matter how early they get here. The earlier the better. In the fall, when mornings are cold, we always build a fire in a fire pit we have for sale. It's nice to be warm on those cold morning with a cup of coffee while taking in the view.

Our Yard Sale ads are always placed in the local Reedley, Sanger, and Dinuba newspapers, as well as The Shoppers. They come out the week of the sale.

We always tell people to come early and bring a truck. Often people wish they'd brought one when they get here. They ask us to store their treasures they've paid for so they can run home and get one!

We encourage the piling of your goodies. This is one of the only places I know of that the more you buy from us, the cheaper it is. We love to haggle. It makes this yard sale more fun! This isn't an event or a swap meet where people want a set price. When one of us says, we are "asking" for a certain price, that means it's time to haggle. If one of us says we "need," that means it's pretty firm but there's a tiny bit of wiggle room and especially if someone's buying a number of things. When we walk with someone to answer questions on prices, we usually write them down on paper. Then we're asked if that's the best price. At the end of the list we go back and reduce it more because the person is buying more than a couple of things. The more you buy, the cheaper it is. And ya' never know what you're gonna find out here!

Creating the Perfect Junk Yard

Junk is a wonderful thing. It has endless possibilities. All those old, rusty things laying around that no one uses anymore can be recreated in some way. They can become part of some junk art for that part of the yard no one visits. Find some old rebar, pound it into the ground, and turn a blue or green bottle upside down on it. The sun will shine through it on sunny days to become a color we don't usually see. It can change the way a person's mood swings when they walk into the garden.

My junk yard used to be a planted row crop garden every year. Two years ago, people were putting new Ag wells in all around us. So far, we've had good water but I stopped gardening to conserve. So, my awesome little garden that put vegetables in our freezer had to stop. It sat fallow for a while just growing weeds. It got so hot that nothing would grow out there anyway. I kept thinking about how I could still use that space.

I decided to clean it up and put in a couple of bathtubs and a wall or two. The first picture is the beginning of the wall. Before spring I hope to have the gravel and stepping stones put down. Then I can add the two old cast iron tubs. They'll be sitting on notched railroad ties under the shade tree. I have Iris growing in an old hog feeder, and more Iris to be replanted in an old rusty BBQ. The Hollyhocks grow so tall they hide the picket fence made from old pallets. They grow in colors of red, pink, and burgundy. They are a good drought plant. I hardly ever water them yet, they just grow taller.

I used all the old doors no one wanted to buy at the last couple of yard sales to complete the wall on the opposite side of where I want to place the bath tubs. They are painted in bright colors with some stencil work. I used discarded gate hinges to keep them all together. The whole door panel is tied to the fence behind. It works out well with the wind out here.

Use old wooden bins for the base of the raised garden, plywood to help the smaller fruit bins sit flat on top, and headboards with footboards to create raised flower or squash beds. Nothing has to match because it's all about using what you have.

Re-Use plastic bags. Plastic bags need to be put down in the bottoms of the smaller fruit bins to help keep the gravel, sand, and potting soil in the boxes when watered. I find that I water less this way because the water stays in the plant bins longer. Now I must keep the Siamese away from the bins. I think I'll lay some chicken wire over the tops of them after I replant.

There's always something to add to a junk yard garden. The funny thing about mine is that I've used all the things people didn't want...until they saw what I did with them. But those things are not for sale now! However, I hope what I've done helps to feed the imagination of others.

RANCH
PICKERS
YARD SALE
On The Blossom Trail

APRIL 27TH, 28TH. 29TH   7AM~3PM

4735 S. Englehart Ave. Reedley 93654

Nearest Cross Street~Central Ave.

Come Early & Bring A Truck!

Furniture for Up-Cyclers or home decor, Craft Supplies, Fabric Remnents, Garden Wares, Tools, Bottles, Dishes, Cast Iron, Rusty Junk, Vintage, Antique, Collectibles, Copper Kettles, Brass Accents, Something for Everybody, & FREE Coffee for EARLY BIRDS.

Preview Available April 26th After 6PM on Instagram:
wahtokecreek

www.facebook.com/ranchpickers/

The next pages are pictures uploaded on Instagram from all our previous yard sales. We hope they give you fabulous ideas. Our Spring Sale will have all kinds of new stuff to set out.

Idea: People always ask what they can do with old bed springs. There is an old bed spring on the end of the cart in the picture above. I use them when replanting a flower bin. Here's what you do. Lay down a large plastic garbage bag, fill bin with rocks, sand, and soil. Then plant the bin. When done, set old bed springs at the corners of the bin, along the sides, and in the middle. It takes about 6-9 bed springs. Then cover with chicken wire. The bed springs hold up the wire. Staple the wire around the outsides of the bin. This will keep the cats from messing in the flower bin. Take the wire off when the flowers or vegetables start to grow up.

wahtokecreek Nice oak tabke and chairs

wahtokecreek New stuff scales n boxes

wahtokecreek New stuff

wahtokecreek $40.00 each

Our past Ranch Pickers Yard Sale Photos may help give an idea of what can be found out here. Some photos may help give ideas to shop owners or vendors on what to purchase for the intent of displaying items for sale. There are endless possibilities

...

wahtokecreek New stuff

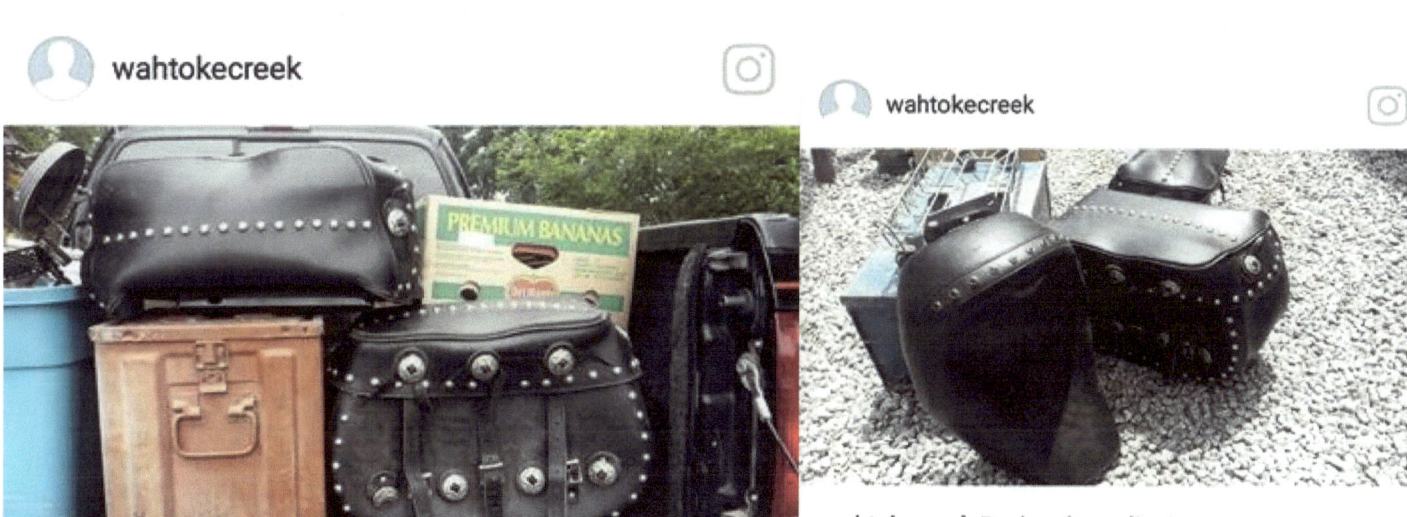

wahtokecreek Panhead goodies!

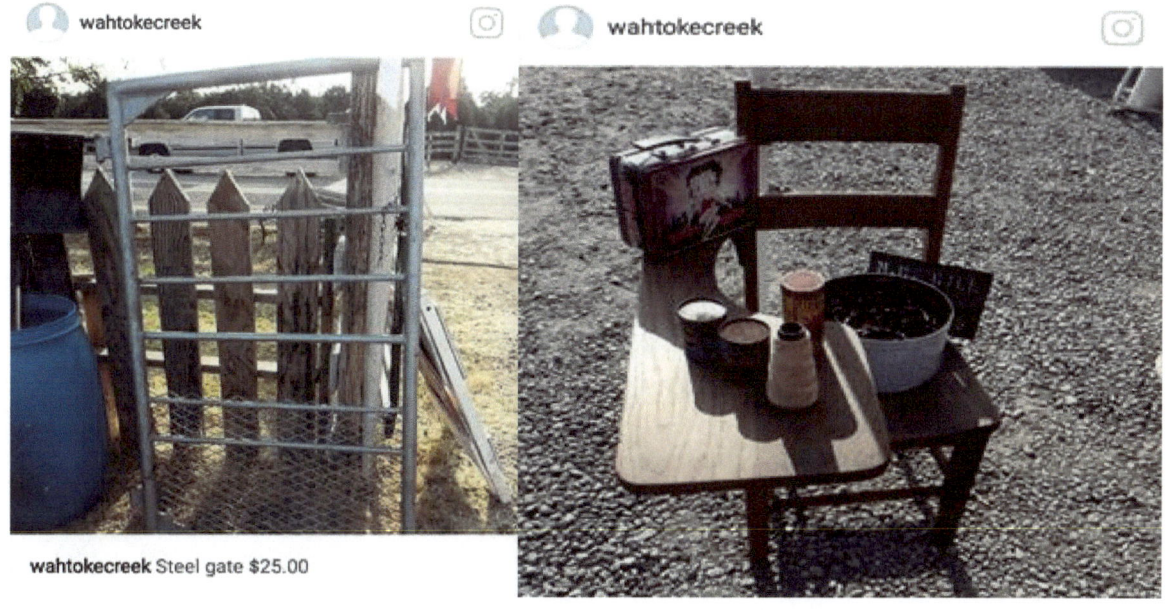

wahtokecreek Steel gate $25.00

wahtokecreek Beautiful antique cabinate $200.00. A steeel.

wahtokecreek Area rug

wahtokecreek New stuff

wahtokecreek New stuff

COUNTRY HOME

ALL MY CHILDREN HAVE PAWS

wahtokecreek Jeans $1.00 EACH

wahtokecreek New stuff

HOME SWEET HOME

wahtokecreek Clean couch $50.00. Shelf $20.00.

wahtokecreek Greeting cards $5.00 a box.

Seen Anything Yet?
Every Sale is Different.

wahtokecreek

wahtokecreek

wahtokecreek

wahtokecreek The whisky train...collectibles

wahtokecreek

wahtokecreek

wahtokecreek

wahtokecreek Window screens $30.00. Go to wahtoke creek antiques for more pictures of how to create with old window screens. Awesome Pintere...

HIGH SPEED JOBBERS DRILLS

wahtokecreek New stuff

wahtokecreek New stuff

wahtokecreek

wahtokecreek

wahtokecreek

wahtokecreek Lg shutters $15.00 each

wahtokecreek

wahtokecreek

wahtokecreek

wahtokecreek New stuff

wahtokecreek New stuff

wahtokecreek

wahtokecreek

wahtokecreek

wahtokecreek New stuff

wahtokecreek

wahtokecreek

wahtokecreek

wahtokecreek

wahtokecreek Update

wahtokecreek

wahtokecreek

wahtokecreek

wahtokecreek All globes and chandelier.

wahtokecreek Wine barrel staves $2.00 each   **wahtokecreek** New stuff   **wahtokecreek** Barrel rings, ladders, windows.

wahtokecreek New stuff

wahtokecreek Fairbanks scale awesome.

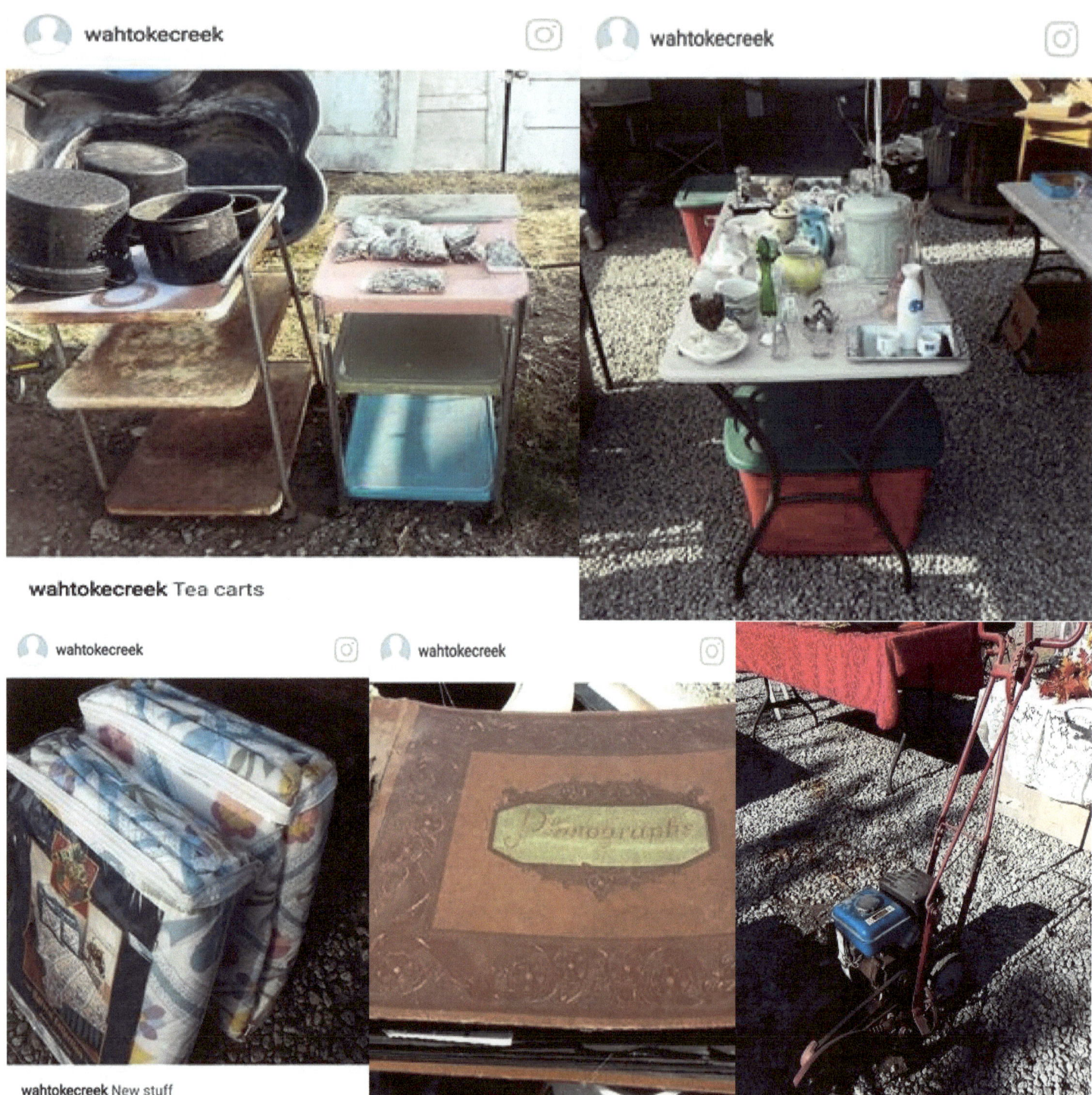

wahtokecreek Tea carts

wahtokecreek New stuff

VISIT our Facebook page at; **www.facebook.com/ranchpickers/**
See our yard sale flyer, get driving directions, add a comment to our
page, see photos, ask a question, and leave us a review.
Thank you!

We want to thank
EVERYONE who comes out
to our Ranch Pickers Yard
Sale. REMEMBER that the
opening day of every yard
sale can be previewed after
6pm the night before. Visit
Instagram and look up
wahtokecreek.
HAPPY JUNKING!